BEFORE YOU BEGIN...

Make sure to download the FREE audio program for this book which comes with your purchase! Just go to

www.slangman.com/audio

then look for your book and enter this code:

E2F34BLQDBTS

Beauty and the Beast

Book Design
and Production:
Slangman Publishing.

Written by: David Burke
Copy Editor: Julie Bobrick
Illustrated by: "Migs!" Sandoval
Translator: David Burke
Proofreader: Emmanuelle Rousseaux

Copyright © 2017 by David Burke

Email: info@heywordy.com
Website: www.heywordy.com

Hey Wordy! and all related characters and elements are © and trademarks of Hey Wordy, LLC.

Published by Slangman Publishing. Slangman is a registered trademark of David Burke. All rights reserved. Reproduction or translation of any part of this work beyond that permitted by section 107 or 108 of the 1976 United States Copyright Act without the permission of the copyright owner is unlawful. Requests for permission or further information should be addressed to the Permissions Department, Slangman Publishing. This publication is designed to provide accurate and authoritative information in regard to the subject matter covered. The persons, entities and events in this book are fictitious. Any similarities with actual persons or entities, past and present, are purely coincidental.

ISBN10: 978-1-891888-17-5

Printed in the U.S.A.

Meet the Author
David Burke

Creator and star of the children's TV show, *Hey Wordy!*, David Burke has been single-handedly revolutionizing the foreign language-learning movement worldwide.

In addition to being a performer of boundless energy and enthusiasm, David speaks seven languages. A successful author and entrepreneur, he has built a thriving international publishing company featuring over 100 books he has written for teen/adults & children. His books have won publishing awards and have sold more than one million copies. David's Street Speak™ and Biz Speak™ series of books and audio programs are used around the world by government agencies, leading universities and major corporations.

Since age 4, David has been a classically trained pianist and uses his musical gifts to compose and perform original songs for his TV series, *Hey Wordy!* which introduces children to foreign languages and cultures through music, animation, and magical adventures. He has also composed, orchestrated, and performed all the music in the audio programs for each of these books.

David's engaging and charismatic persona became a fixture on broadcast entertainment channels around the world, such as CNN and the BBC. David and his work have been highlighted in many major publications, including The Los Angeles Times, The Chicago Tribune and The Christian Science Monitor.

"This series teaches everyday words that occur in your child's life, as well as terms having to do with politeness, greetings, family & friendship."

David Burke

French vocabulary taught:

bague = ring
beaucoup = very much
bête = beast
bon = good
bonjour = hello
cheval = horse
cinq = five
collier = necklace
déjeuner = lunch
gentil = kind

jardin = garden
Je t'aime = I love you
midi = noon
moche = ugly
monsieur = sir
quatre = four
rose = rose
s'il vous plaît = please
six = six
voyage = trip

The words in **green italics** throughout this fairy tale are words you've already learned in the previous level! Do you still remember what they mean?

from Cindellera (level 1)

amoureux = in love
au revoir = goodbye
beau = handsome
belle = pretty
chaussure = shoe
de rien = you're welcome
épouse = wife
fête = party
fille = girl
grande = big

heureuse = happy
maison = house
méchante = mean
merci = thank you
minuit = midnight
moment = moment
pied = foot
prince = prince
robe = dress
triste = sad

from Goldilocks & The Three Bears (level 2)

bébé = baby
bol = bowl
chaud = hot
cuisine = kitchen
deux = two
dur = hard
fatiguée = tired
fauteuil = armchair
froid = cold
lit = bed

maman = mama
mou = soft
ours = bear
papa = papa
petit = little
porte = door
promenade = stroll
table = table
trois = three
un = one

fille ←

beaucoup ←

Once upon a time, there was a *papa* who had an eldest (daughter) named Julie, a middle **fille** named Tessa, and a youngest **fille** named Belle. He loved them (very much). While preparing

to take a long trip, he asked each filee, "What can I bring you from my viagem?" "I'd like a ring to wear on my finger," said Julie. "I'd like a necklace to wear around my neck." said Tessa.

voyage

bague
collier

3

S'il vous plaît

rose

But Belle, who was the most *belle* of all said, "Please. I don't want a **bague** to wear on my finger or a **collier** to wear around my neck. All I want is a rose." He replied, "You shall

each receive your gift." "Oh, *merci*!" said each *fille*. Then their *papa* mounted his horse, and they shouted "Have a good voyage, *papa*! **Bon voyage**! We will miss you **beaucoup**!"

cadeau
cheval
bon

As he rode off, each *fille* shouted again, "*Au revoir, Papa! Au revoir!*" until he was out of sight. Days later, it was time for him to return. So he first stopped to buy a **bague** for his eldest

fille to wear on her finger, a **collier** for his second *fille* to wear around her neck, but he waited to get closer to his *maison* to look for a garden where he could find a **rose** for

jardin

Belle. After a few hours, he saw a magnificent **jardin**. He got off his **cheval**, walked into the **jardin** and picked a **rose** that was the most *belle* he'd ever seen. At that *moment*,

the *porte* to the *maison* opened and a *grande* [beast] came out and ran toward him. "Who stole a rose from my *jardin*?" exploded the *grande bête*. "S'il vous plaît, [Sir]!" said the *papa*.

bête

monsieur

"**S'il vous plaît**, don't hurt me, **monsieur**. I promised my *fille*, Belle, I'd bring her a **rose** as a **cadeau** after my long **voyage**. It was just ONE **rose** from your **jardin**!" "It's still

stealing!" said the *grande* *bête*. "I will spare your life if you bring me the *fille* you speak of by (noon) in (six) days. Here she will live the rest of her life." Naturally, the

midi
six

papa was very *triste* by this request, but he promised he'd return with Belle at **midi** in **six** days. As he arrived home, each *fille* rushed out to greet him. He gave them each

the **cadeau** they'd asked for. Each *fille* was very *heureuse* and shouted, "*Merci* **beaucoup**, *papa. Merci!*" "*De rien!*" he replied. But he was still *triste* because he had to tell Belle

13

je t'aime

about the promise he'd made with the *grande bête*. "Belle, I love you **beaucoup** and want you to be *heureuse*. But I must tell you what I have done..." Her *papa* went on to

explain what had happened that day and about the promise he had made. He warned her about how [ugly] the *grande* **bête** was, but Belle felt responsible because the **rose** was a **cadeau**

moche

she'd requested. So, she agreed to go. **Six** days passed quickly and it was time to leave. Each *fille* was very *triste* to say *au revoir* to Belle, but they understood that she had no choice.

So, Belle and her *papa* mounted the **cheval** and rode off. They arrived at exactly **midi** as instructed. Belle and her *papa* got off the **cheval** and approached the *maison* of the *grande* **bête**.

Bonjour

The *porte* opened slowly and they walked in. "Hello!" said the *papa*. "*Bonjour*!" But there was no answer. As they walked in, they saw a *grande table* in the middle of the *cuisine* filled with food.

It looked like someone was having a *grande fête*! Just then they heard a deep voice say, "**Bonjour**. This lunch is especially for you. **S'il vous plaît**, enjoy!" Not wanting to be impolite, they began

déjeuner

eating the magnificent **déjeuner** before them. And so many desserts! Belle was so excited and already busily counting them. "... four, five, **six**. **Six** different, wonderful desserts!

quatre
cinq

She counted them again just to make sure, "*Un*, *deux*, *trois*, **quatre**, **cinq**, **six**! It was true! **Six** delicious desserts all for them! They had never seen a more wonderful

déjeuner in their lives! Suddenly, they heard footsteps approaching. There he was – the **grande bête** himself. Indeed, he was truly **moche**. Scared, Belle said, "**Bonjour**,

monsieur and *merci* for the delicious **déjeuner**." "*De rien*," replied the *grande bête*. He seemed very kind toward Belle. Her *papa* was permitted to come visit her every week

gentil

which made her very *heureuse*. He gave Belle a kiss on the cheek, mounted his **cheval** and said, "*Au revoir*, Belle. **Je t'aime beaucoup**!" and rode off back to his *maison*. At that *moment*,

the **grande bête** turned toward Belle and said, "**S'il vous plaît**. What's mine is yours. I will return every day at **midi** to see you." He then quickly ran off, leaving Belle alone.

Because he was so **gentil** toward her, Belle was no longer afraid, and was even *heureuse* when he came to visit at **midi**. Every day, they laughed more and more

and enjoyed sharing stories with each other. But one day, the **grande bête** didn't arrive at **midi** as usual, so Belle went to look for him. She walked outside into the

jardin and there he was lying on the ground lifeless. Belle cried, "Oh, why did you have to die? **Je t'aime**! **Je t'aime beaucoup**!" She gave him a kiss on the cheek and

suddenly, right before her eyes, he awoke and was transformed into a *beau prince*! He explained to her that an evil magician had changed him into a *grande bête* and

only the kiss of a *fille* who was truly in love with him, and the words "**Je t'aime**" could change him back. The next day at **midi**, Belle became his *épouse*, and they all lived happily ever after.

Now you're ready for Levels 4 & 5!

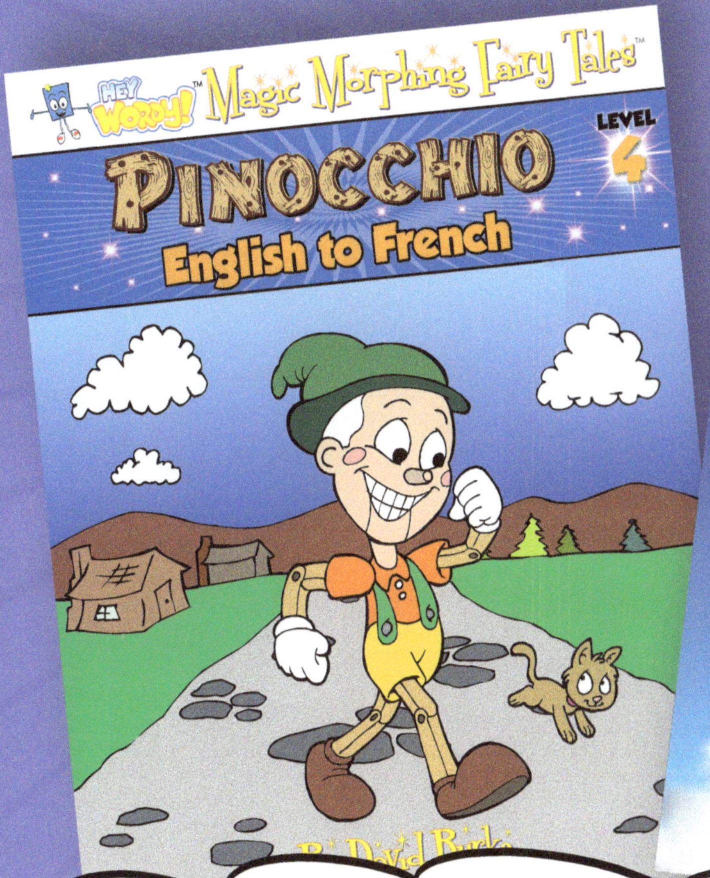

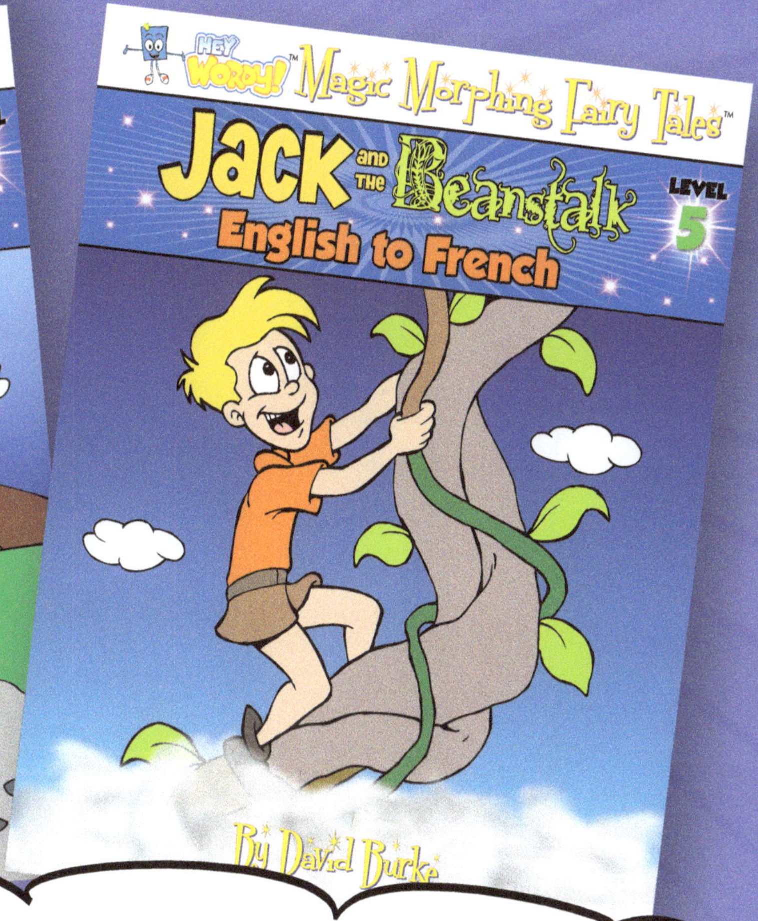

Levels 4 & 5 contain the words from Levels 1, 2 and 3 plus all NEW words!

For more HEY WORDY! products, visit...

www.HEYWORDY!.com